GET THE H*LL OUT OF MY HOUSE

A CAUTIONARY TALE OF AN EMPTY NESTER'S WORST NIGHTMARE

WRITTEN BY **ALAN KATZ**
ILLUSTRATED BY **CRAIG ORBACK**

Skyhorse Publishing, Inc.
New York

Skyhorse Publishing books may be purchased in bulk at special discounts for sales promotion, corporate gifts, fund-raising, or educational purposes. Special editions can also be created to specifications. For details, contact the Special Sales Department, Skyhorse Publishing, 307 West 36th Street, 11th Floor, New York, NY 10018 or info@skyhorsepublishing.com.

Skyhorse® and Skyhorse Publishing® are registered trademarks of Skyhorse Publishing, Inc.®, a Delaware corporation.

Visit our website at www.skyhorsepublishing.com.

10 9 8 7 6 5 4 3 2 1

Library of Congress Cataloging-in-Publication Data is available on file.

Cover design by Daniel Brount
Cover artwork by Craig Orback

Print ISBN: 978-1-5107-5931-2
Ebook ISBN: 978-1-5107-5939-8

Printed in China

I really love you as a child,
but I want to be alone with my spouse.
So pack up your shit, go rent a truck,
and get the hell out of my house.

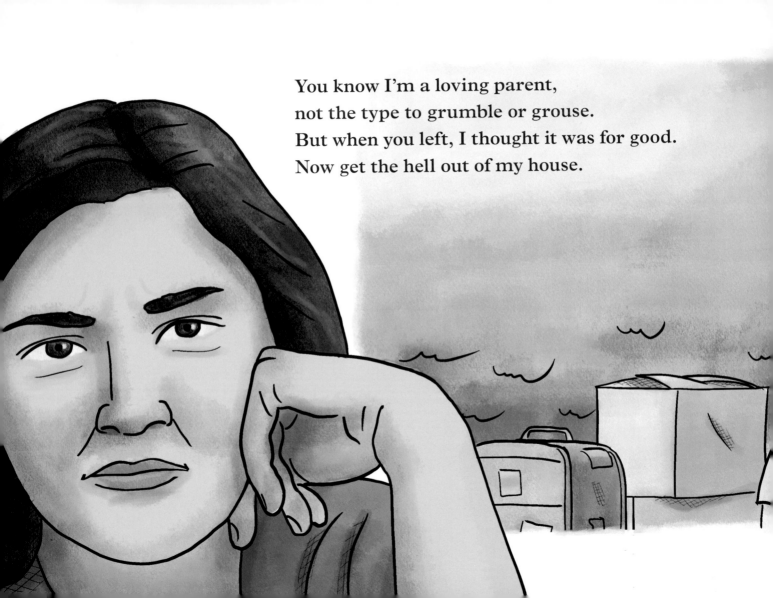

You know I'm a loving parent,
not the type to grumble or grouse.
But when you left, I thought it was for good.
Now get the hell out of my house.

College

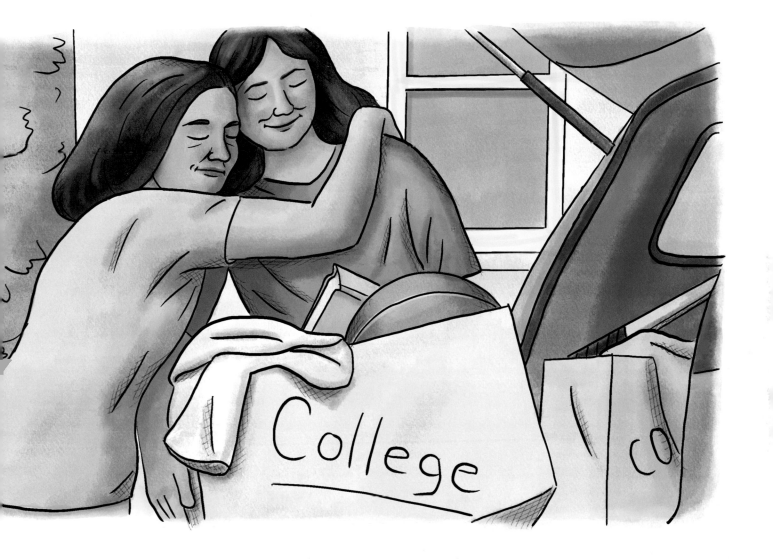

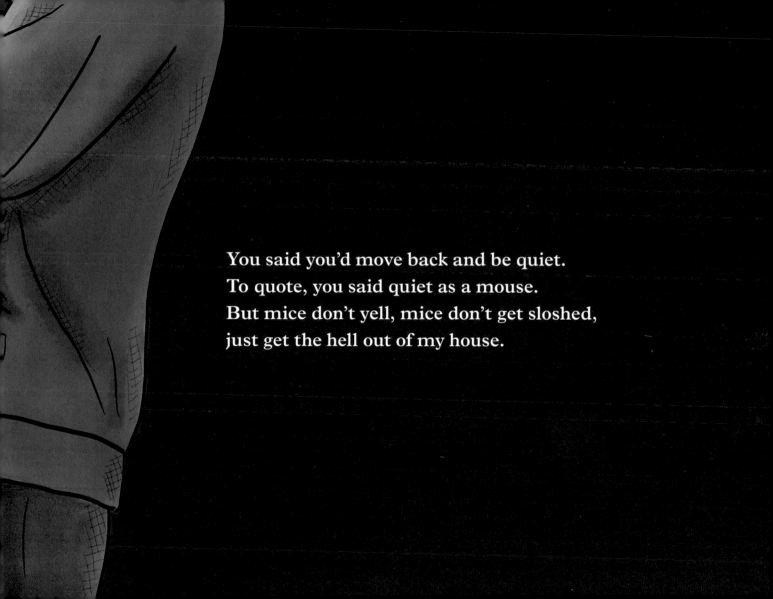

You said you'd move back and be quiet.
To quote, you said quiet as a mouse.
But mice don't yell, mice don't get sloshed,
just get the hell out of my house.

You were a boarder for so many years,
(not including nine months of maternity).
You asked to come back, you said it'd be brief.
But B-R-I-E-F don't spell eternity.

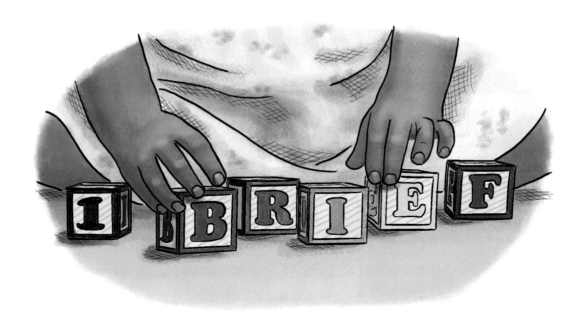

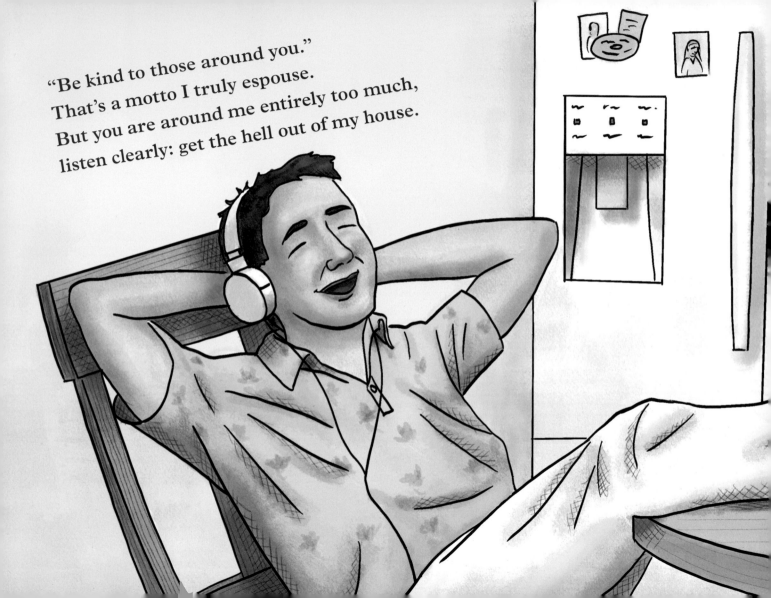

"Be kind to those around you."
That's a motto I truly espouse.
But you are around me entirely too much,
listen clearly: get the hell out of my house.

POPS

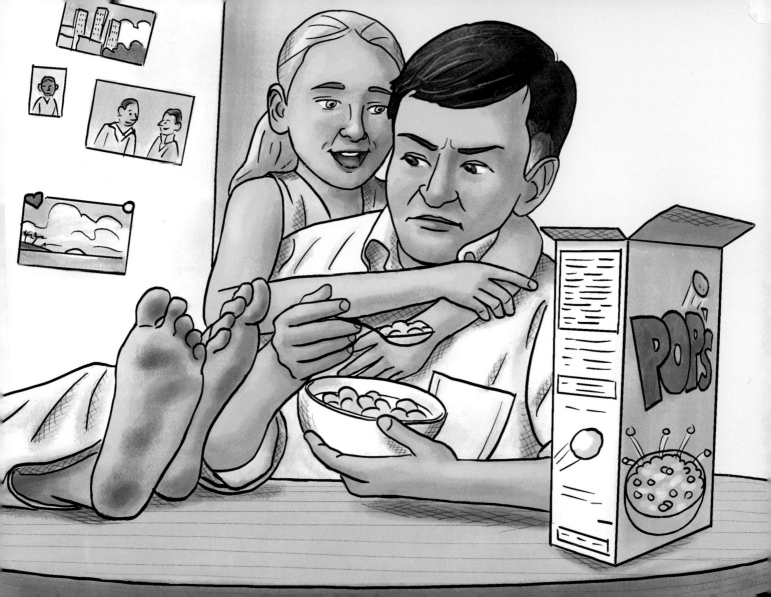

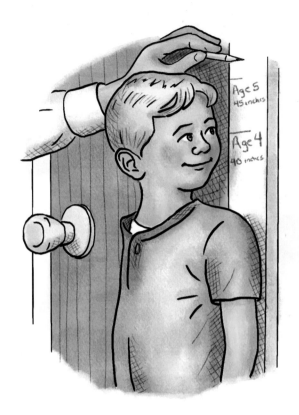

You were sure cute when you were little,
but that cuteness fades when you get tall.
So ferret out your phone under that huge pile of crap,
and dial 1-800-GO-UHAUL.

Age 4

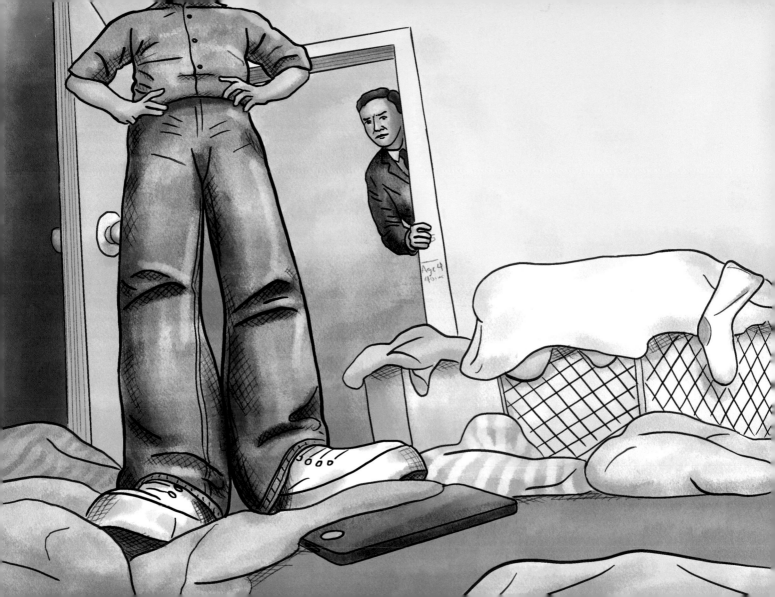

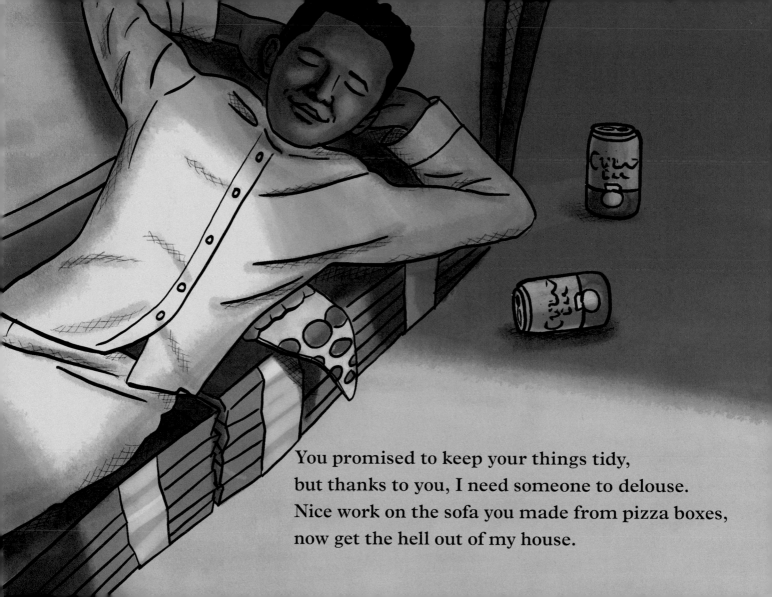

You promised to keep your things tidy,
but thanks to you, I need someone to delouse.
Nice work on the sofa you made from pizza boxes,
now get the hell out of my house.

To put our clash of temperaments in musical terms,
you're heavy metal, I'm Johann Strauss.
I'm quite composed, your life's decomposing.
Tempus fugit; get the hell out of my house.

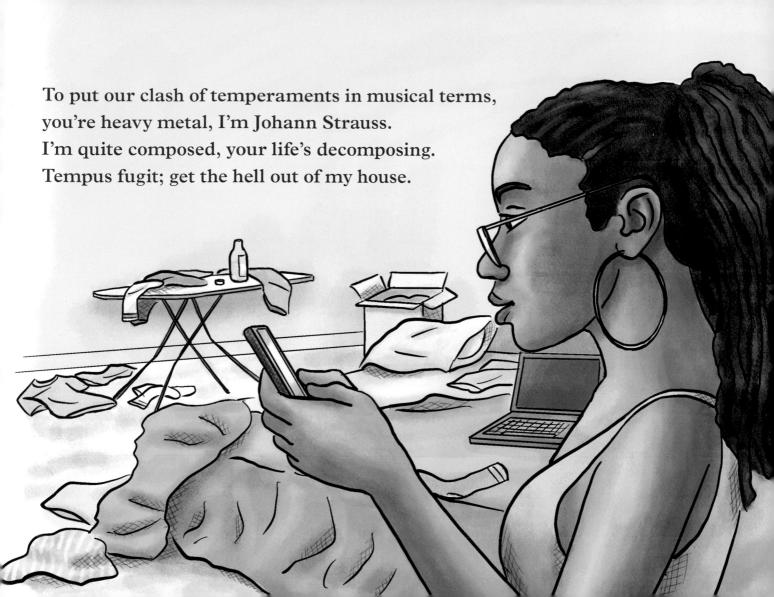

MOVING OUT

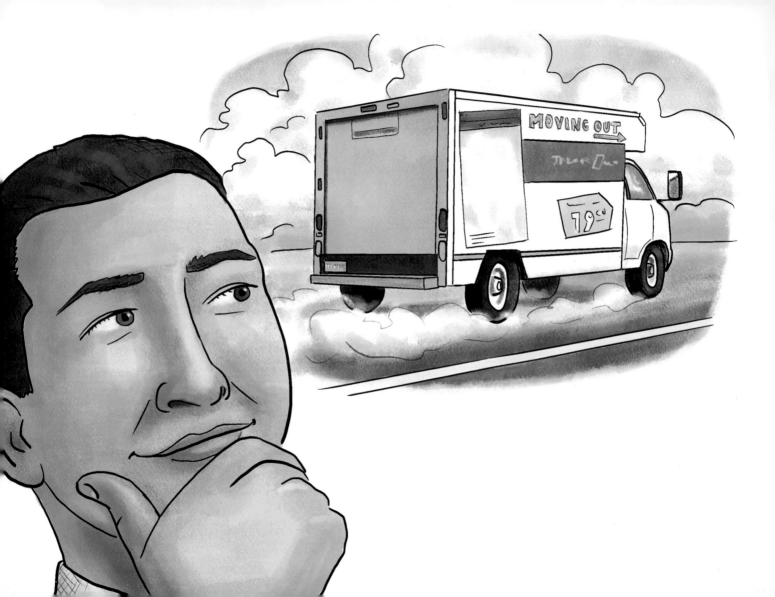

Move. Move. Move. Move. Move. Move.
Now please read that last line again.
Great news! The minute that you're all cleared out,
I'm getting a shiny new den!

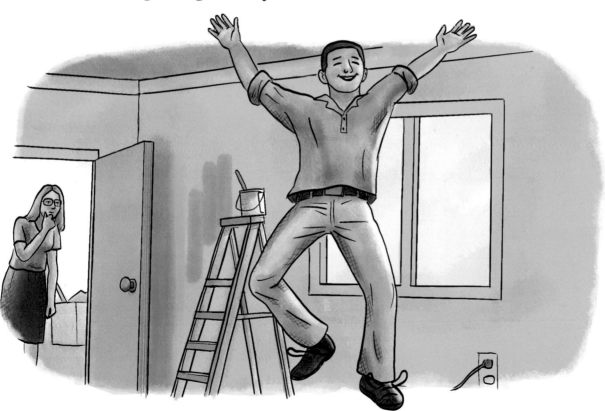

I know a lot of millennials are back with their parents.
In fact, I read it's fifty-two percent.
But that's a majority I don't want to be in.
Go somewhere and start paying monthly rent.

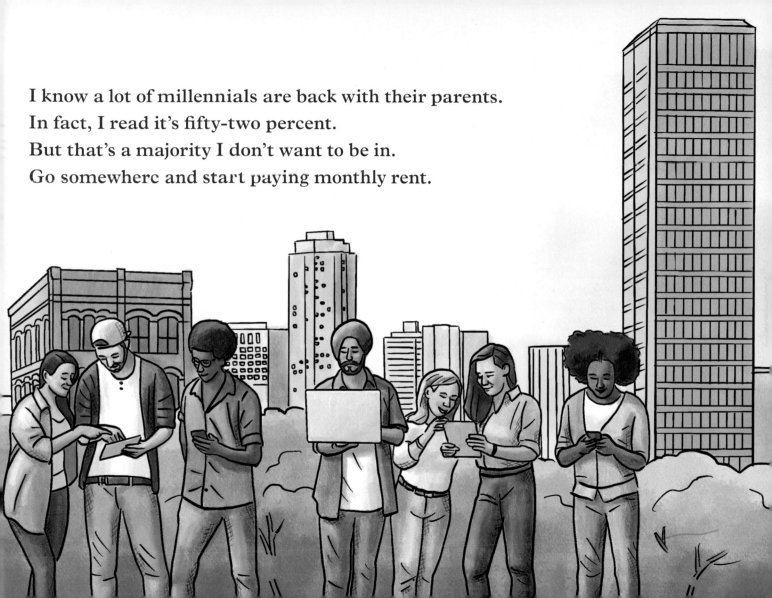

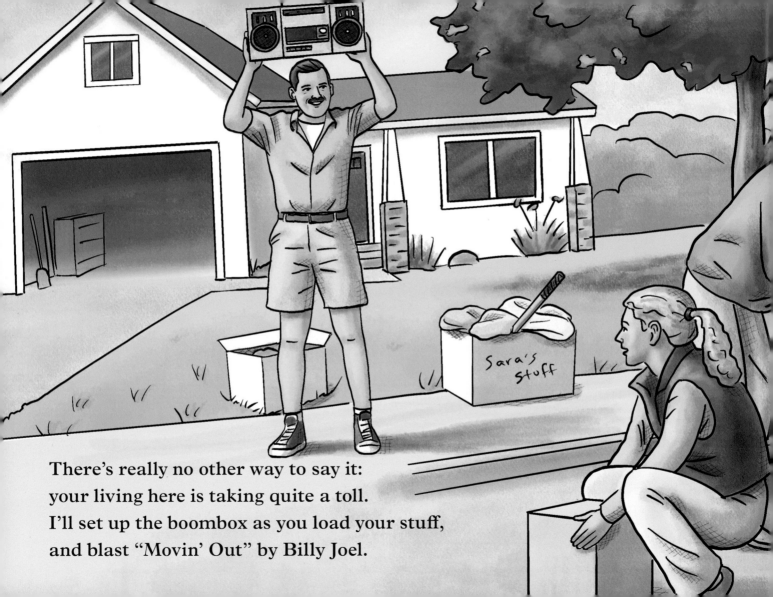

There's really no other way to say it:
your living here is taking quite a toll.
I'll set up the boombox as you load your stuff,
and blast "Movin' Out" by Billy Joel.

Sara's

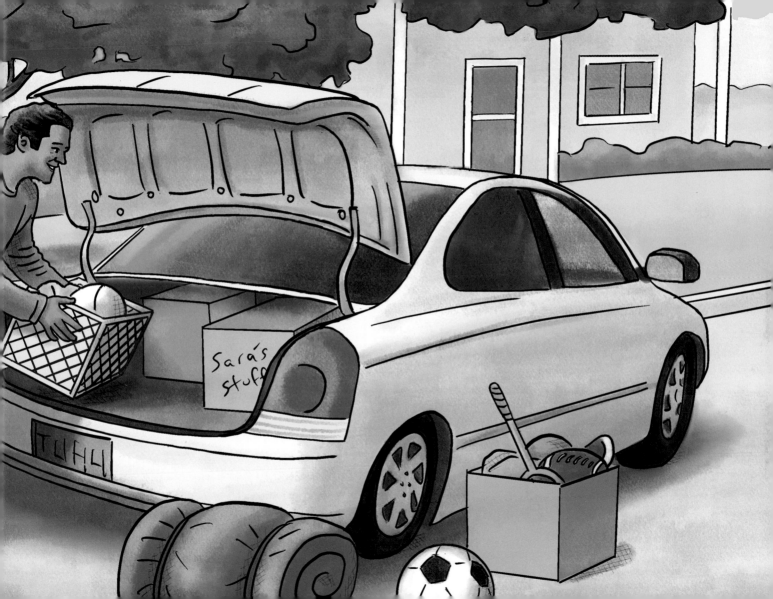

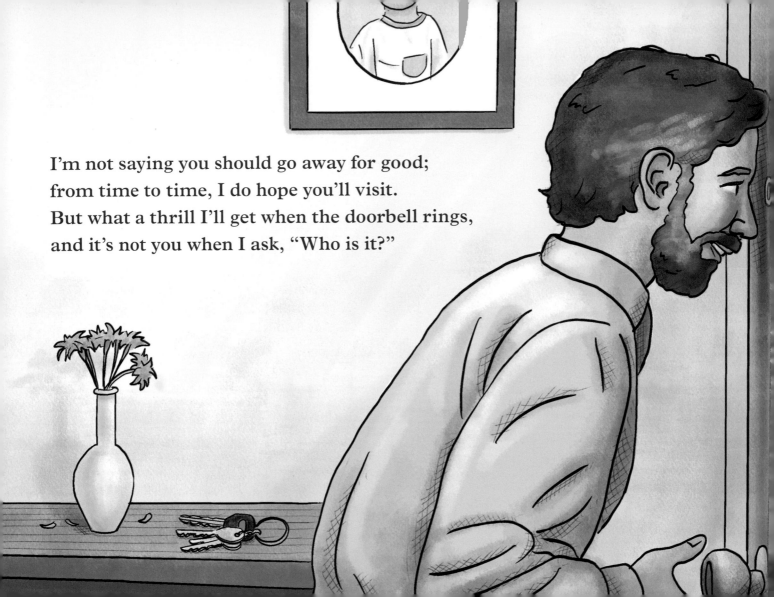

I'm not saying you should go away for good;
from time to time, I do hope you'll visit.
But what a thrill I'll get when the doorbell rings,
and it's not you when I ask, "Who is it?"

I fed you, I clothed you, we played, sang, and danced.
You know I've loved you deeply, without doubt.
At birthdays, the best parties on the block is what we threw,
and now, my dear, it's time to throw you out.

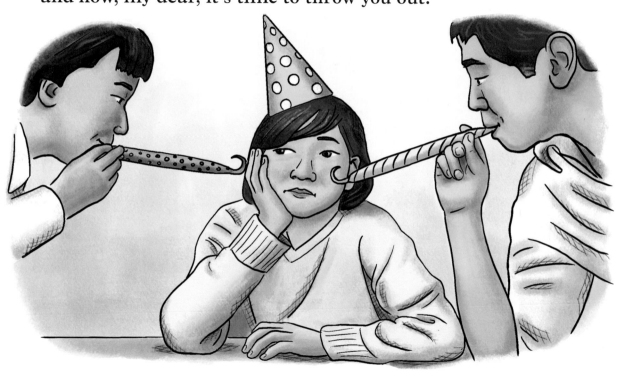

college
College

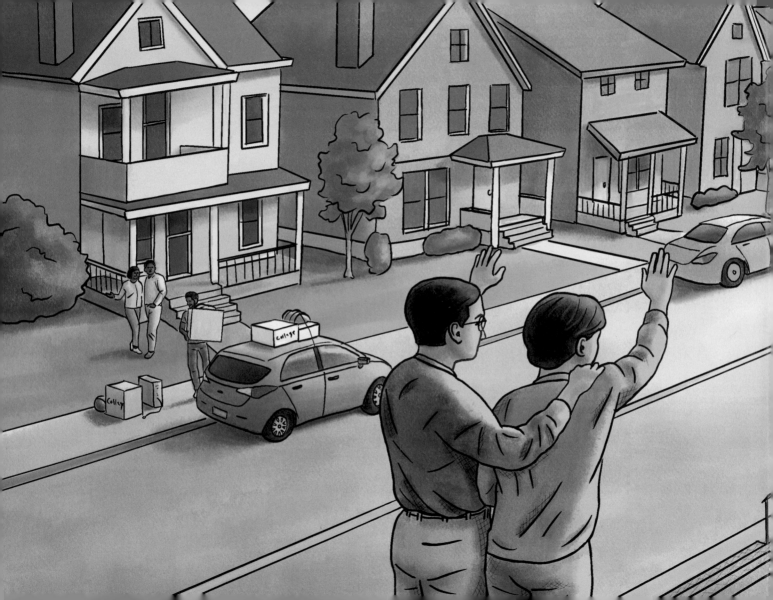

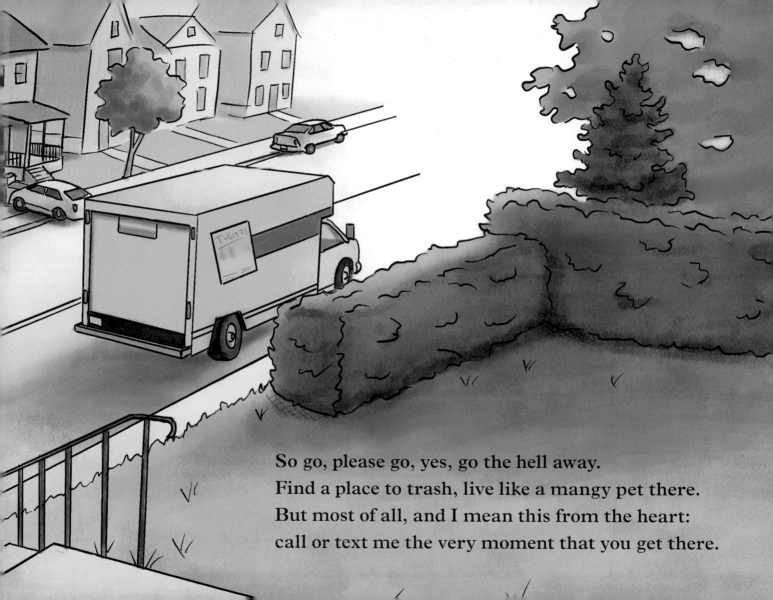

So go, please go, yes, go the hell away.
Find a place to trash, live like a mangy pet there.
But most of all, and I mean this from the heart:
call or text me the very moment that you get there.

INCOMING CALL

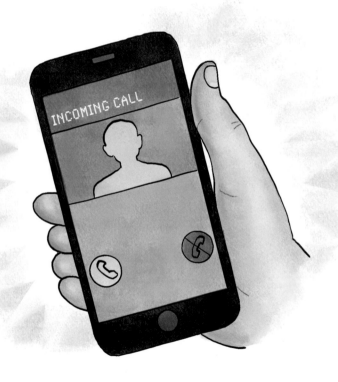